# *Nostos*

Palimpsest Press
1171 Eastlawn Ave.
Windsor, Ontario. N8S 3J1
www.palimpsestpress.ca

Printed and bound in Canada
Cover design and book typography by Ellie Hastings
Edited by Jim Johnstone

Palimpsest Press would like to thank the Canada Council for the Arts and the Ontario Arts Council for their support of our publishing program. We also acknowledge the assistance of the Government of Ontario through the Ontario Book Publishing Tax Credit.

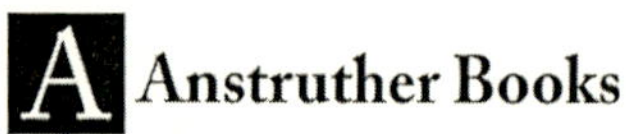

Canada Council for the Arts
Conseil des Arts du Canada

Canada

LIBRARY AND ARCHIVES CANADA CATALOGUING IN PUBLICATION

TITLE: Nostos : poems / Tracy Wai de Boer.
NAMES: De Boer, Tracy Wai, author.
IDENTIFIERS: Canadiana (print) 20250175452
Canadiana (ebook) 20250183048

ISBN 9781990293931 (SOFTCOVER)
ISBN 9781990293962 (EPUB)
SUBJECTS: LCGFT: Poetry.
CLASSIFICATION: LCC PS8607.E2218 N67 2025 | DDC C811/.6—DC23

# Nostos

poems

Tracy Wai de Boer

# Contents

## nostos



## epilogue

*for all the i's*
*journeying to become an I*

## Nostos

A theme used in Ancient Greek literature in which an epic hero returns home by sea. The return affords the hero greatness, as such a journey is arduous and involves being shipwrecked and enduring trials and hardships. *Nostos* is not only about returning home physically, but also about the hero's retained or elevated identity upon their returning home.

## Nostalgia

From the Ancient Greek, *nostos,* meaning return home or homecoming; and *algos,* meaning pain. The literal translation of nostalgia being painful return home or painful homecoming.

# algos

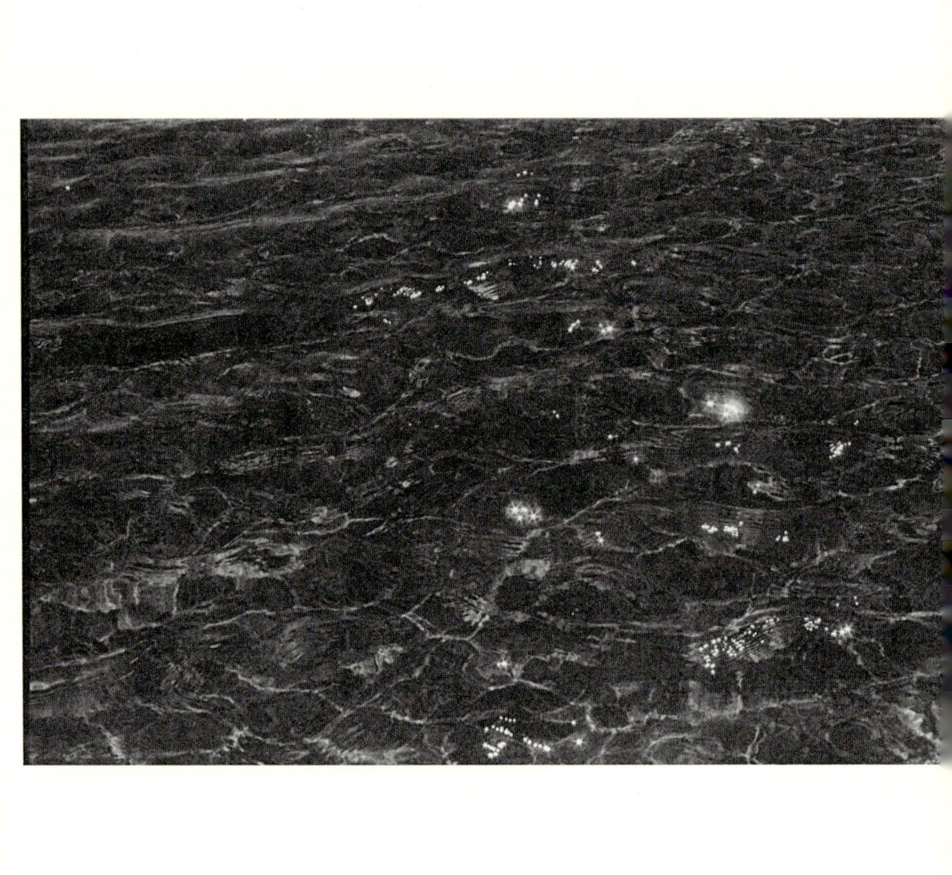

## At Sea

Before,
i had never known power.

In the wake of water cut
i'd turn away
from distant sound and fullness
only to hear it again –

once i saw him from above, strength in body yet somehow
beyond
warm-blooded freight train

i only know by name.

And all the while i,
a toy boat,
balanced on the wind
so precarious a sigh might capsize me.

## Origins

i came from the sea –
first on fins then on fours
learned to walk upright.

The we before me grew the knack,
through wobbly waters and uneven tides
followed a thread tied to the shore and built
a life to hang onto
          when waters got rough.

We crossed the Atlantic to be here
or maybe it was the Pacific?

Mom only ever said *gong gong* (or *bak bak*?)
shared a boat with a soy sauce man –
an oil man with a rich black liquid far more precious.

Or maybe i dreamed it.

She said things like that
when she didn't have the answer.
Spun stories
from silk, wrapped around her neck loosely,
carried by the wind as she walked.

## Baleen

i taste red
and all teeth from my mouth.

Surely felt them wriggle loose,
held on by strings
to each his own umbilical cord –
*the nerve!*

Once i read teeth mean decision
or indecision?
Or was it death? Or did i make it up?

Once i was told
those who become unpregnant dream of lost teeth

as certain as an unholy god curses each of us
to disassemble ourselves.

Surely sometimes teeth break –
and there i am, left with shards of them
to spill like a puzzle.

Then maybe, i mean surely,
in each place
i'd grow new ones

learn to inhale through long stranded teeth
like combs made of bones.

And what would i say if no one was listening?

i will follow
but how can a toy boat survive at sea?

## Pinhole

Is it true we were blessed to live in a world of perfect balance
yet cursed in our inability to see it?

Pain pulls you through a pinhole
pierced through the heart
in one airless pinprick.

i follow it all the way.

Bet they didn't know you could crawl through that hole,
like a magnet on the other side, two weights holding in place.

The rest is endless expanding outer space
from the other side.

## Double

That night,
i dreamed a dream of double love.

There, all the parts had somewhere to call home.

i dreamed a dream of double love
where all the parts had someone to call home.

Someone to call home as someone calls
me home.

i only listen out of one ear.
The other can't hear you, as an ornament or vestige
of another language.

## Twin

That i might find a mirror image
where softness is sharpened to a point.

It's my mistake – i thought we were a matching set.

But really,
we're apples and razor blades,
helium and handshakes only meeting momentarily in the hour
between my going to bed and her waking.

It's my fault –

that i let drop your hand to tie my shoe
stole sugar cubes from your mouth

called you before i knew the right words.

Fault,
have i created a monster?

## Mammalian

What is better than love
but to be in the hands of a professional?

i dreamed of him again from ocean's edge
warm-blooded freight train with a heart to hold a carriage.

Went home one day to find everything
not as i left it.

i told you this one before.

We went back, who were you?
They tell me you run the world –
only i'm not so sure.

What's bold in daylight is boyish at night.
Here's evidence,
a gift i tried to take back.

To me alone, he said,
remember the mechanical in the mammal.

To me alone, the impulse
at once to dominate and dissolve.

## The Poem Is the Thing Cast Into Water

To resurface later.

# Another Language

The instinct to return
to an empty well

again
again

and hope by some magic it
might be filled

against dry rock,
buckets

when
and when.

# Lullaby

Just give me a room of my own
and pour oil over my hair

feed me fruit and cheese,
tea with honey
and i'll never ask for anything.

Wrap me in sheets of lavender
   burn incense   and holy wood
paint my walls white,
a shrine to my laziness.

Please –

just let me lay
down feathers   pulled from baby birds
so that i might have somewhere to sleep.

Leave the lights low
sing to me that old tune
the one my mother used to sing

of picking tea leaves
from Chinese hillside
in a language i don't speak
but understand the meaning of.

# Cleaning I

Don't ever ask after my morning apple cores
or
while you're gone i'll shred your sheets
with seamstress shears

like a cat who leaves a carcass,
not a gift but a warning
unless you welcome the teeth.

Don't mention the dishes
or
anything for that matter
don't commit domestic nonsense with me.

# Cleaning II

Scolded for something forgotten,
this might have been the last of the laundry
the final clean cup, perched, the top of the rack.

Here, i'll cook the peaches – just say the word,
i'll usher away your orange peels,
leaving them at the alter with the incense,
so the gods know we are accounted for.

## Doppelgänger

i woke this morning to your doppelgänger,

her first time petting a dog
fingers extended into spiders

i saw you and your daughters
your mothers in one,
unfolded.

Why did you leave when you did?

i wasn't ready but there's no arguing –

i didn't see you that summer or the summer before,
as i had each and every as memory serves

those heavy aired days strung together
with Cantonese.

You showed me the mark we shared
through the language we did not.

i saw you only once after you left,
adorned regal, a queen of continents.

## Champion

When he crossed over what separated us,
i wasn't looking for anything but a way home
but a champion,

a chair
        in a crowded room,
a gift
        held just for me.

*A champion*, they tell me,
is one
who rises above
the weight of circumstance.

Endings come too soon –
think all the gutted fish in the sea,
think all the places burned before their time.

And so, we slide ourselves into
soft spaces of safety, peeled and dried –

being held in place,
suspended
we go into hiding.

## Drought Years

You took me to the zoo that day
and even though we fought later

there in the shade, my head in your lap
as you read your book,
we still brushed up against peace.

The hippos, *equus flumine*, you said,
which means *river horse*.

*i know i know*
submerged but for nostrils

i thought of us that summer,
sprawled out each night
trying to beat the heat.

i stroked your hair, marvelling
its length, the curl
we went back twice
to watch tamarins groom each other.

The pettiness and necessity of it all
as turtles fought over fish flesh.

## Void

As if it were a game,
we stayed until midnight –
pushed boundaries
we knew not to cross

pretended to be tough
pretended not to be
played soft – exposed my belly
watched your face closely

(a void)

today i asked, *what is cruelty*
unoccupied, containing nothing.

# Baleine

It began with the dream upon brain jelly,
of water, of night –
warm-blooded freight train

though submerged, i called out –
but all that spilled from my mouth
was a language
not my own.

Your legs stuck out like thumbs, as evolution's afterthought
hitchhiking across the sea.

In another i am transactional
to serve and exist
in tight circles of permission.

At ocean's edge i am all held in place
by the joint impulse to dominate and dissolve
or perhaps domesticate?

Is there some way i can stay?

# Desire Is a Four-Letter Word

Wanted left wanting –
it wasn't me but my Shadow.

Mournful call, i forgot how it felt
that you were there in my Shadow too.

Deserted pathways,
the phone that broke the wall.

My father said,
*You'll spend half your life wishing*
*and the other half denying.*

But, Shadow, does it have to be me too?

My sense and superpower are the same
too much always too much.

A hand on my throat is care or carnivorous
a wishful thing
a cup balanced on my knee.

Desire is a four-letter word
meaning *want.*

Desire is a four-letter word
meaning *most.*

Desire is a four-letter word
meaning *much.*

Desire is a four-letter word
meaning *more.*

## Uninvited

There you are again
uninvited

why won't you just leave
me alone

stop floating by
where you don't belong.

## Loosely

Am i loosely put together?

My body fails me
equal parts propelled
and betrayed by.

If i can put a bone out of place by sleeping
there's someone else to blame.

It's the pain
but as i said,
you learn to like it.

## Stasis

Not a gasp,
fixed
steady          in places
you don't want it to be.

Can't you force flow?

Blood, burgundy as period sludge,
forgotten in body parts
over dark water.

Birds fall from the sky
as wind ceases to move
air collapses,
unable to go beyond –

fixedfluid.

Still, i sit steady,
wait.

## Nostalgia

On Mondays i wake, feel blue – soft and vulnerable in
squishy places.

i get like this. Find my way down a well-trodden path, feel silly
all over again looking in windows long since abandoned.

Here i ache from the inside out – wonder where everyone went
already it's the future – as if i always knew it would be.

Am i cheating happiness when i come back here?
Afterall,

*nostos*
means homecoming
*algos*
means pain.

From the outside looking in, i forget the texture of each
memory
all of them sad and sweet.

At the other end of the lane, i look up to find
my mother is an old woman
my baby sister, all grown.

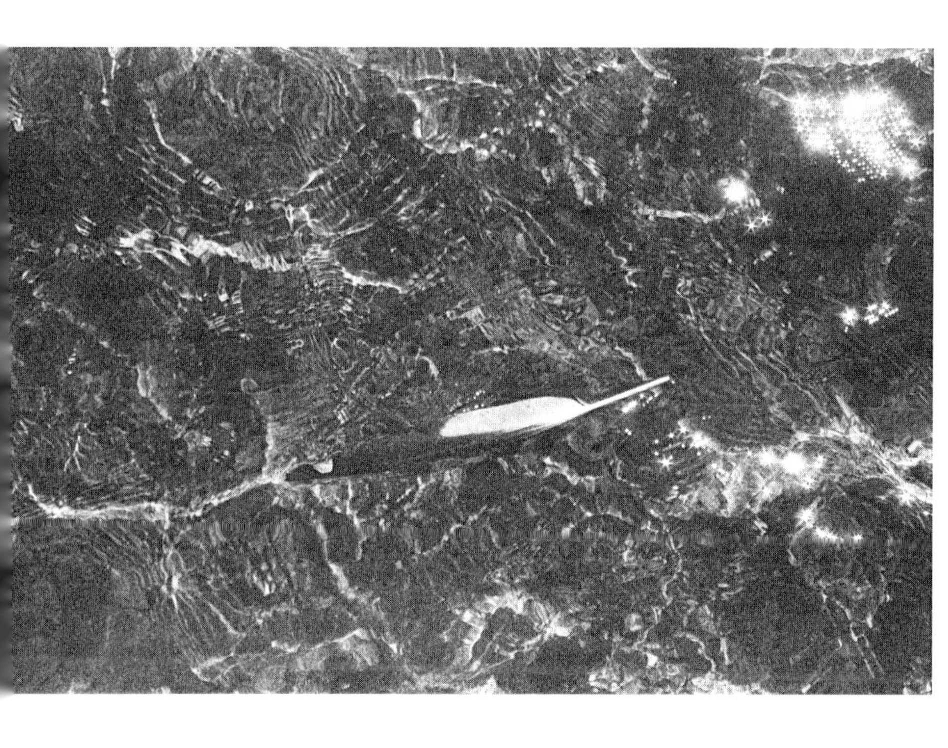

nostos

# Standby

Did i ever tell you about the first time i saw the ocean?

It was Sarah's birthday. Dad took us for a day trip – he worked for the airline. We flew standby. i carried a pocketknife that was nearly taken and he put it in the car before we boarded,

*it would be a shame to lose that one.*

There on the other side, we went to the aquarium, but all i wanted was to taste the sea. At end of day, we stepped slippery rocks and without tumbling too far, found a small pool to drink from. But i didn't take a big enough gulp, barely lapped fingers touching the tidepool.

i'd wait years to return.

## Baleine Baleen

i run my fingers through your teeth
stiff as horsehair
untangle each strand
so that we might breathe freely.

## Proximate

Is adulthood replaying childhood
using only proxies?

Everyplace i felt alone – or everyplace
i felt foolish i revisit
only to find things are different.

Could i superimpose one over another
hear that same song again
and see you were only human?

i've watched this movie before,
all the actors have changed.

Can we go back
but not back –
can we go forward by going back?

Play this over again
backwards
listen for secret messages.

## Cleaning III

*A good relationship has a shared epistemic infrastructure*
i thought –

but it drifted by in fragments
and escaped my grasp.

What is life when we look too closely –

this morning i wondered if there really is
such a thing as forward

not in a cynic's way, but watching the waves
go out and come back in –

i'm not sure forward is the right frame.

eat, release, eat again
break, heal, break again

i cook, i clean,
i come

if i'm lucky i remember to do so slowly.

## How to Spell *Bread* in French

The first time i lost all my teeth i was a child.

i learned then even the bones in my face
are impermanent.

When i was seven
i lost "permanent" teeth when i fell down the front steps
(face first)
incisors versus concrete.

Now i bite into ice cream without wincing
(a superpower no one asked for).

At twenty-nine and seven months
i hit my head, lost all the words inside,

knocked C5 or T5 out of line like dominoes
sheared vertebrae as books stick out from the shelf.

i thought by summer i'd be up again
it should only take 3 months
then 6
then 12
then 24
then 36

There's no way i could do this for years now –
at some point i stopped counting.

Once i asked my mother how to spell, *bread* in French
p – a – i – n
she said.

*Yeah, but how do you pronounce it?*

You have experienced .

In times, on high alert,
your senses focus to a point
to hunt
to look
to search
to survive

this is your birthright.

We beings learned how to be –
there is nothing shameful in this.

Brilliant bright light expands,
the edges of your body and spirit meet to form a new thing.

That focused strain you once knew is no longer
the threat, away, he who brought it, away.
Yet your ears still perk up. They always do.

Animal wisdom is always called upon,
you sharpen the blade but

tonight, it is just the wind
the scrape of a tree,
the branch outside your window.

# Lost and Found

Who knew power could hold my hand so gently?
or that strength could bow down to softness?

Words aren't always able
misplaced like keys in couch cushions –
swept back.

Instead of drawing into disgust,
the thing to do is have a look around.

Arrive honest
to find what was lost last time –
the words we didn't have,

all sharpness worn smooth.

i scramble down,
*here they are!* i've found them
held up glossy in sunlight and
slick with last night's sweat.

## City of Jewels

Mother said,
*you can have it all*
                        *but not all at once.*

How i grew to hate these words.

But they take up new meaning
in time

i never got to act out then –
have dessert for dinner    or know the cause
of the pinprick pains
which besought my fingers, heart, solar plexus.

i knew only what i knew,
grew solemn before my time –

she, a free spirit, solarplexusstrong
the kind who married thrice,
fed camels orange peels among desert sand.

*Tell me the one with the white dress again,*
i'd ask while falling to sleep.

*The one with the army tank, the soldiers,*
*the kubutz*

*the biggest fish you caught at the lake –*
*(bigger than all the men who woke early that day)*

*fruit in the shower*
*with the James Dean lookalike –*

*the giant rat who startled you and two strangers*
*in New York City –*

*or the one where you kissed the basketball-playing lawyer –*
*he was dressed as Humphrey Bogart under the bridge.*

## Happiness for Anxiety

Just now i wrote that wrong –
*anxiety for happiness*

i've been having trouble word-finding
slow to the trigger
speak not the word, grasp for it, finding it not there.

i wonder if this is normal forgetting
acceptable slowness
or is it something
*...else?*

Here, i don't know
i am anxious – no – i am actually excited
Mom always said they were two sides
                                        of the same blade.

Is it that i can't tell which is which?

Maybe you'd feel bad for me, bemoan my loss
but now i find within myself a rich amusement park,
a playground in reverse colours.

Who would have thought there'd be so much
more in here?

i started to dream in French
the phrases formed on their own
in my mind, Matthew broke *la clavicule*
*ça va?*

wonder if my brain jostles like a bag,
dropping some elements,
shifting others to the front.

*Oh look, the word is missing*
am i misplaced or out of shape?

Instead, i take handfuls of the words (as pebbles)
those out of arms reach
the ones i can't find inside –
i cast them into the waves, cackle to the wind.

## Little Key

Matthew took a spill around the corner
fell from his bike tumbled over handlebars
into the hot city streets that June.

Rush houred to hospital the cab ride bumpy
teeth tense, he sipped through the pain.
In emergency, we waited seven hours,
hungry, laughed the whole time.

Later,
he said he felt the vibration of music against the bone
the two halves ground together as if mismatched gears –
even the texture of water hurt.

The sex was silly and slow.
All the while he slept at an angle
(easier on the pain)

we shopped for button-downs and i bathed him
wedged paper towel to wipe sweat
from his armpits all summer.

The bones met again and merged on their own
as we watched over weeks on x-ray.

*But now my nipples are unaligned,*
he told the doctor, whose assistant stifled a laugh.

## Safe Passage

It took her some time.
Father's mother passing into the afterlife –

one waits for an expectant mother to fully dilate
the thinning of the veil.

Her death more drawn out than Father's father
who passed swiftly in the night

sitting upright at his desk
a cup of tea gone cold, unspilt.

*A heart attack,* they said.
Father laughed,
*He didn't even have the sense to clutch his chest and fall forward.*

*No* –
he would never have allowed himself
to be found that way.

## Sea Glass

Between pebbles i found words we tossed
overboard, a decade ago.
There was such a sense of motion i got dizzy
just reading them.

We spun into what we thought was infinite
only to stumble and scrape knees –
we were never to blame, though
                    like i thought we were.

We swam through it all with ease
collapsed on the shore suntanned
   and sand-covered    drunk with the day.

You still visit me in dreams
always short on time –

for a few months you were each day's first and last
   a confidant or an unripe lover.

i don't swan dive like i used to
rather dip toes to test waters
but there were times in recent years, all grown
i thought    *if i saw you now, i'd dive back in*
break the surface for an afternoon and
remember
who we used to be.

## At Dinner

After the swim, we are hungry.

She recounts her life in decades rather than days now
and we laugh.

The rice is cold, but the water is warm.

# Word Origins

I.

Volatile from the Latin,
*volare* to the Middle English
for "a creature that flies."

What's that got to do with it?
to fly off the handle?

II.

Paranoid from the Greek,
*para*, meaning irregular
*noos*, meaning mind.

III.

Aggressive
from the Latin,
*aggredi*
attack.

## Messenger

i looked up from the page to ask,
                    each time he answered

all the while regretting –

through him, the beauty each answer unfolds
a message in a bottle
carried over time, unrolled in my eager hands.

A keeper of the words, he held them until –
                    speak soft in my ear
while i drift between worlds
made for me, this place of keeping.

## I or i

i debate whether to capitalize i
or any of the words at all –
when i do it all looks wrong
as if a stranger wrote it.

i read articles – "English capitalizes I"
many other languages don't
when i sought why
they said because i could not stand alone –

too easily lost in a sea of letters.

Why i and not I?
Jim and i discussed this
*i like the anti-establishment bent*, i said
but really – i'm not sure.

Audre Lorde removed the y from her name
she didn't like how it hung below the other letters.

i like the thought of being a particle amongst other particles
a little piece, adrift, surrendered to that same sea.

That I holds himself above the rest
but i is in the flow of it –
and if not here, where i rearrange letters
to make nonsense but somehow make meaning,
then where?

i once wondered if i too should remove the y from my name
and be but a trace.

Later Michelle tells me lowercase poems relate to oral tradition
– as if one were speaking them.
Maybe i am straining to listen as it pours in through one ear
perhaps it is spoken – and here i am hearing
without time for the *I*'s or *Why's* of it.

## Muchness

Is it god i find
within myself?

A certain type of loneliness,
                                        unavoidable.

People make for more loneliness
i'm made up of muchness
much hair
much body
much feelings
much thoughts
much tears
much laughter
much longing
much need
sometimes so much, i spill out
in all directions, a painting without a frame
lacking containment.

Here the veil between living and dying.

Each edge takes shape,
sand pushed by hand into lines
where soft grains become glass,
pulverized.

with the edges taking shape,
i see what i only pictured before –

i too could grow thumbs and horsehair teeth,
fins from what was left for dead.

My body filled then with saltwater
the edges are only waves
                    worn ragged.

## Unburden

i knew it some
not intimate
as a well-worn path home
but newly familiar –
a rearranged grocery aisle,
the body of a fresh lover.

## Vestiges

Don't you see?

i was here the whole time
waiting, and awaited
listening closely
hoping you'd come home.

i've been told not to use *-ing*
in poetry, too weak.

What may i do or not do?
Your voice is a footprint, a trace.

Isn't the *-ing* the becoming
the roving of the verb as it unfolds in infinite evolution?

i found all my teeth in the sand
the baby ones, the ones i outgrew.

## Come Home

Come, let me put on my white dress,
the one you asked me to make.

Let me comb my fingers
through your greying hair –

i can see where you keep your wisdom.

## Foremost You Are a Tongue

You are a tongue and you are ears but before that
you were fleshdust come home after a rainy day –
mortified to have found a human form, fragile
and covered in tiny hairs.

To be a wife is to be the sea
    forever in motion
yet steady.

Formed by the tide, we call
from the telephone mounted on fastidious loops

like tacky trains we leap over cliffs
in bounded braid rope, clipped wings and thorny crowns.

She calls out in her language,
but in the time it takes to translate, we have already gone.

i missed you the first year
that first rotation, as we danced around the sun.

It wasn't until i came home and heard the phone ringing,
that i remembered,
*i am her.*

My love, you are no mind reader –
made to believe
you were capable of such inhuman feats.

Here I am, a tongue, and ears, and tiny hairs.

# epilogue

## To Be Strong in The Face of Wanting

I find myself, as I often do, so full of wanting.

Desire is a wish, a space to unfold –
mouth open, palms facing upwards.

A sense of reverence for what is Holy –
embodied, maybe.

Who will let me play, free and open in that space?

Let me crawl on the floor for you – bring you the news,
undress for you
cake with honey, warmed.

A chance vanished – so overcome.
If only there were a way to know – but isn't wanting half the fun?

Come,
lay your head in my lap,
my fingers at your forehead, in your hair –
so nimble but certain
let my hands find you.

Let me help, let me help.
Let me be, let me be.

Let me in –
let me draw circles in the sand for you.

## Plunge

Submergence in things past
will never do.

What is it *to plunge*?

To swim wholehearted as to return
to cast off
to remember
          the joy of beginning
the first blanket
to leave the bad day behind.

To give into what was always coming.

# Notes

[i]Summarized from the Wikipedia entry on “nostos” with additional discussion with Matthew, who holds a Ph.D. in Classics and Ancient Philosophy.

Word origins from Latin and Ancient Greek arose from discussions with Matthew, who is proficient in these languages. Other translations and etymologies were sourced with the help of the Internet or completely made up.

An early incarnation of my thoughts on the entity, “baleine bleue,” a French blue whale, was published as “the blue whales” in my chapbook, *maybe, basically* with Anstruther Press (2020).

All images were captured on 35mm cameras belonging to my parents, my mother’s Canon FTb and my father’s Nikon FM-1. The Canon captured experimental imagery my mother created when she was in art school. The Nikon captured much of my childhood.

The photographs were captured on 35mm black-and-white and colour negative film stocks. Some images were intentionally underexposed while others were converted to black and white.

# Acknowledgements

Thank you, Palimpsest Press, for believing in and supporting the entirety of the vision for this book. Thank you to Aimee, Ellie, and the entire team for your generosity, support, and most of all your patience, as I embarked on this debut collection.

Thank you to my editor, Jim Johnstone, for his enduring warmth, enthusiasm, care, and critical eye. I'm grateful to you many times over. You made this book more of a book than I could have alone. It's always a pleasure to work with you and learn from you.

Thank you to the Ontario Arts Council for funding this work through the Recommender Grant Program. I cannot emphasize enough the lasting value of arts funding.

Thank you to the Banff Centre of Arts and Creativity for providing me and so many others the space to explore, discuss, and develop. I am grateful to have attended the Late fall Writer's Residency in 2023 and workshop a draft of *Nostos*. Thank you to Klara du Plessis for providing valuable encouragement and feedback at that residency. I also acknowledge, with gratitude, the Carolyn Tavender Endowment, which provided the funding for me to attend.

Thank you to *Petal Projections* for publishing earlier versions of "Doppelgänger" and "Foremost You Are a Tongue."

A special thank you to Puneet Dutt, for pointing out to me in 2018 that I was writing poetry, and I should do something about it.

Thank you to Nick for the many conversations, and for helping me refine the questions and the answers.

Thank you to Matthew, for your support in all the ways. I am grateful every day for your place in my life, for our love and friendship, and for the critical and artistic conversations shared over many years and many walks.

Thank you to my precious family, for being weird, independent, brilliant lovers of living. You are my life's guiding force and foundation. Your verve and ferocity are present in everything I do.

Thank you to the many other poets, artists, friends, and passersby who helped me uncover the ways of doing it or not doing it.

Finally, thank you, Reader, for being here. Thank you for buying this book, for borrowing it, for finding it in a little free library, for salvaging it from a free pile, or in whatever way you picked this up and held it in your hands.

# About the Author

Tracy Wai de Boer lives by the ocean. She is a writer and artist whose creative work spans poetry, experimental photography, and mixed media. Tracy is the author of the chapbook, *maybe, basically* (Anstruther Press, 2020) and coauthor of *Impact: Women Writing After Concussion* (University of Alberta Press, 2021). *Nostos* is her first full-length collection of poetry.